weird but true!

DINOSAURS

NATIONAL
GEOGRAPHIC
KiDS

weird but true!

DINOSAURS

300
DINO-MITE FACTS TO
SINK YOUR TEETH INTO

NATIONAL GEOGRAPHIC

WASHINGTON, D.C.

THE **SPIKES** ON *STEGOSAURUS'S* TAIL WERE AS LONG AS A THREE-YEAR-OLD KID.

5

Antarctica HAD **lush forests** WHEN **dinosaurs** ROAMED THERE.

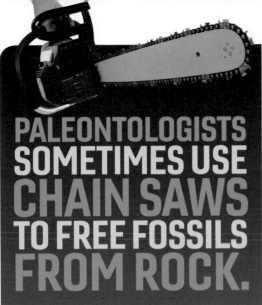

PALEONTOLOGISTS SOMETIMES USE CHAIN SAWS TO FREE FOSSILS FROM ROCK.

The largest dinosaur eggs could hold about six gallons (23 L) of liquid.

Scientists **once thought** the heavyweight *Brachiosaurus* had to **live in water** to support itself.

MEAT-EATER
TRATAYENIA ROSALESI
HAD **SHARP, SERRATED CLAWS** AS LONG AS **BOWLING PINS.**

SCIENTISTS FOUND A FOSSILIZED PIECE OF **T. REX POOP** IN CANADA THAT WAS THE SIZE OF A **LOAF OF BREAD.**

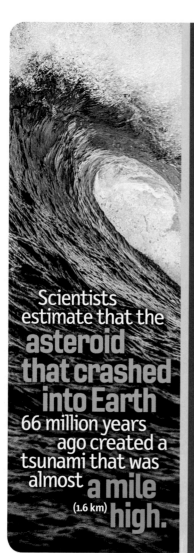

Scientists estimate that the **asteroid that crashed into Earth** 66 million years ago created a tsunami that was almost **a mile** (1.6 km) **high.**

You can **buy** a **full-size** *T. rex* replica for **$100,000.**

Visitors to
**Dinosaur
National Monument**
in Colorado and Utah, U.S.A.,
can only see dinosaur fossils
on the Utah side.

Fossilized
Triceratops
horns
were originally
MISTAKEN
for those of an
oversize bison.

12

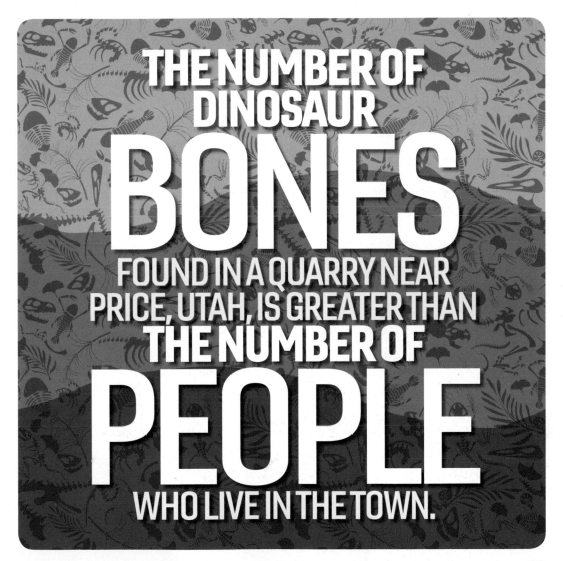

THE NUMBER OF DINOSAUR **BONES** FOUND IN A QUARRY NEAR PRICE, UTAH, IS GREATER THAN THE NUMBER OF **PEOPLE** WHO LIVE IN THE TOWN.

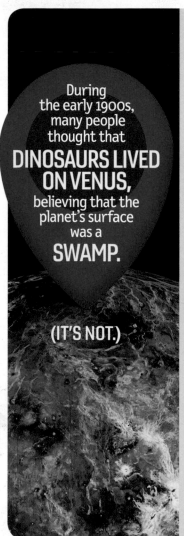

During the early 1900s, many people thought that **DINOSAURS LIVED ON VENUS,** believing that the planet's surface was a **SWAMP.**

(IT'S NOT.)

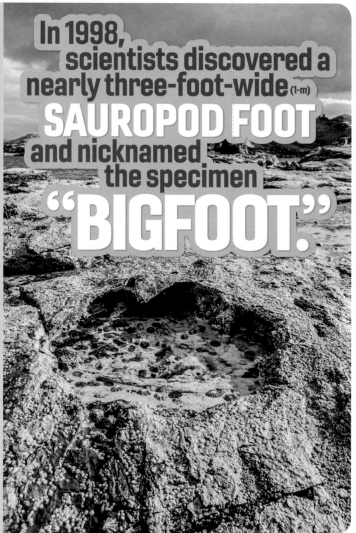

In 1998, scientists discovered a nearly three-foot-wide (1-m) **SAUROPOD FOOT** and nicknamed the specimen **"BIGFOOT."**

A MODEL *T. REX* IN DRUMHELLER, ALBERTA, CANADA, IS **FOUR TIMES TALLER** THAN A **REAL *T. REX*.**

In 2015, the actor **NICOLAS CAGE** turned over a dinosaur fossil **HE'D BOUGHT FOR $276,000** when he found out it had been **STOLEN.**

KIDS CAN TAKE DINOSAUR-THEMED YOGA CLASSES.

You can buy a WEDDING RING partially made of DINOSAUR BONE.

Gastonia had **FOOT-LONG SPIKES** JUTTING OUT (0.3-M) from its back and shoulders.

Some kinds of tyrannosaurs have been named "frightful lizard," "powerful terror ruler," and "monstrous

murderer."

A DUCK-BILLED DINOSAUR FROM WESTERN CANADA HAD A COMB ON TOP OF ITS HEAD, LIKE ROOSTERS DO TODAY.

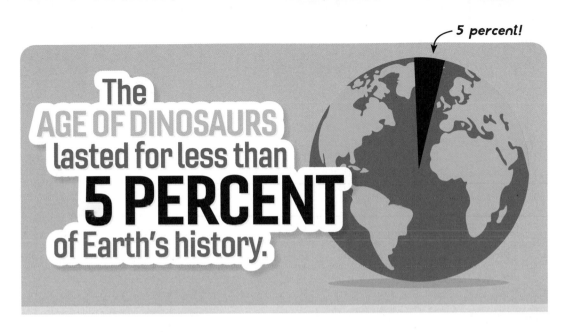

5 percent!

The **AGE OF DINOSAURS** lasted for less than **5 PERCENT** of Earth's history.

The Sicilian boy's name **Dino** has nothing to do with **dinosaurs;** it means **"little sword."**

During the 1997 Macy's Thanksgiving Day Parade, a Barney the dinosaur balloon **crashed** into a streetlight and **deflated.**

T. REX'S JAW WAS AS LONG AS A SEVEN-YEAR-OLD KID.

Researchers named *Cretalamna bryanti,* **A SHARK** that lived alongside the dinosaurs, after famous University of Alabama football coach PAUL "BEAR" BRYANT.

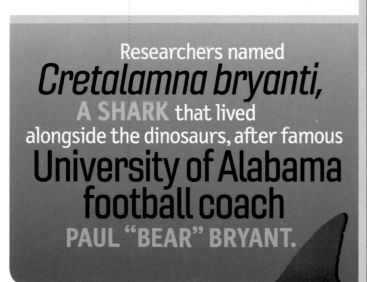

HIGH WINDS
SHAPED A TREE IN NORFOLK, ENGLAND, SO THAT IT LOOKED LIKE A **T. REX.**

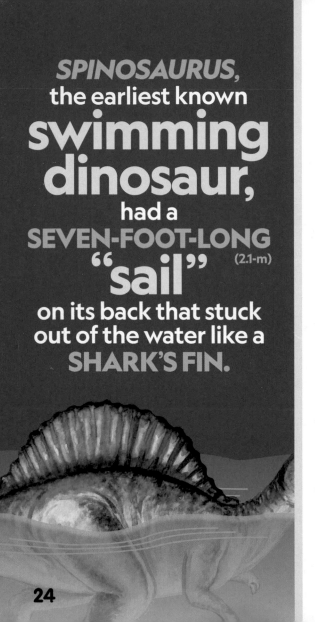

SPINOSAURUS, the earliest known **swimming dinosaur,** had a **SEVEN-FOOT-LONG** (2.1-m) **"sail"** on its back that stuck out of the water like a **SHARK'S FIN.**

THE **WOLLEMI PINE TREE** THRIVED ALONGSIDE THE DINOSAURS; **FEWER THAN 100** MATURE TREES ARE **ALIVE TODAY.**

Scientists think that *TSINTAOSAURUS*, a duck-billed dinosaur, had a hollow, domed **CREST** on top of its head.

25

Triceratops
HAD THREE HORNS ON ITS HEAD,

BUT
Kosmoceratops
HAD 15!

Scientists raised **CHICKENS** with fake, **STRAP-ON TAILS** to see how *T. rex* may have **WALKED.**

Hawaii doesn't have any dinosaur fossils; the islands are **not old enough.**

THE MOTHER'S DAY QUARRY FOSSIL SITE in Montana, U.S.A., was discovered on Mother's Day and is full of **FOSSILS OF YOUNG SAUROPODS.**

Like baby humans, *Psittacosaurus* **crawled** before it walked.

The **Crying Dinosaur** is a **rock-climbing route** in the Superstition Mountains in central Arizona, U.S.A.

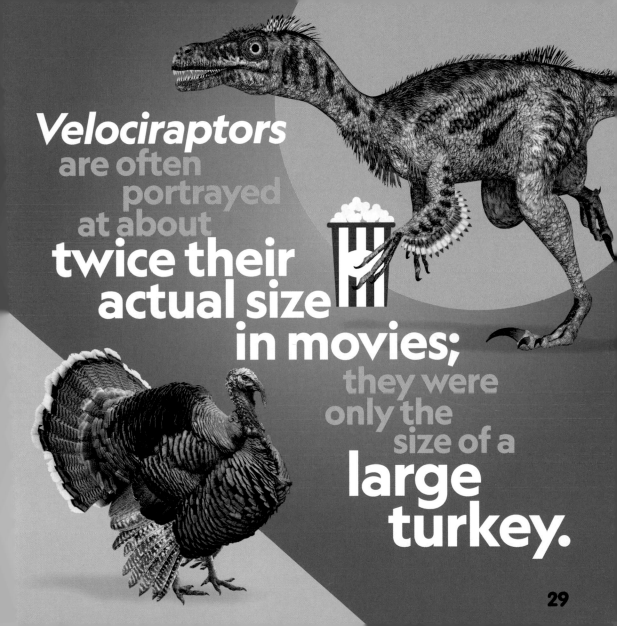

Velociraptors are often portrayed at about **twice their actual size in movies;** they were only the size of a **large turkey.**

29

DINOSAUR BONES HAVE BEEN FOUND ON **EVERY CONTINENT—** INCLUDING ANTARCTICA— BECAUSE WHEN DINOSAURS EVOLVED IN THE TRIASSIC, THE **CONTINENTS WERE CONNECTED.**

A paleontologist once argued that **HUNGRY DINOSAURS** ate so many eggs that all dinosaurs **WENT EXTINCT.**

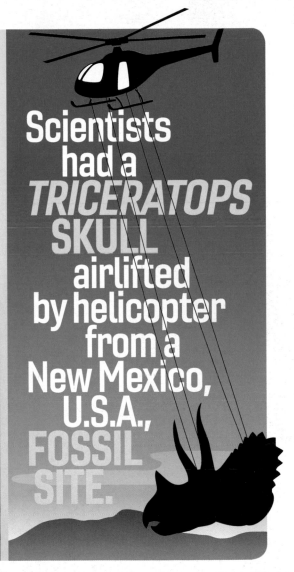

Scientists had a *TRICERATOPS SKULL* airlifted by helicopter from a New Mexico, U.S.A., FOSSIL SITE.

Beatles musician **Ringo Starr** played a **caveman** named Atouk in a dinosaur movie.

Patagotitan mayorum, the largest animal to have lived on land, weighed as much as **10** African elephants.

In the 1960s cartoon *The Flintstones,* the Stone Age family had a pet dinosaur.

Caihong juji, a duck-size dinosaur, may have been covered in **rainbow-colored** feathers that **sparkled** like a **hummingbird's.**

Some scientists think **Allosaurus** used its **head** as a **hatchet** and then slashed prey with its teeth.

Allosaurus couldn't fly; but, like a bird, it had **hollow bones.**

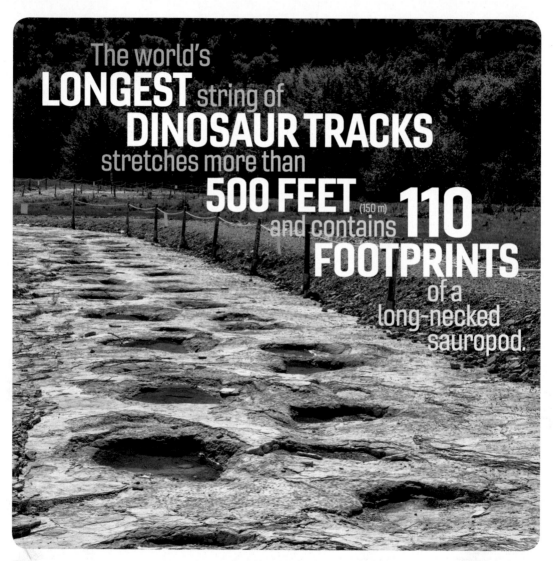

The world's **LONGEST** string of **DINOSAUR TRACKS** stretches more than **500 FEET** (150 m) and contains **110 FOOTPRINTS** of a long-necked sauropod.

IN THE 19TH CENTURY, A FARMER IN EASTERN BRAZIL **LOOKING FOR HIS LOST FLOCK** DISCOVERED DINOSAUR TRACKS; SCIENTISTS LATER FOUND TRACKS FROM MORE THAN **80** DIFFERENT SPECIES.

Plant-eating *Edmontosaurus* had **diamond-shaped teeth.**

Smugglers listed a box of dinosaur **fossil skulls** as **"shoes"** on the **customs form** to ship them from Mongolia.

IN *JURASSIC PARK*, THE SOUND OF *T. REX* shaking its prey CAME FROM A RECORDING OF A Jack Russell terrier playing with a rope toy.

The first scientists to study *Therizinosaurus* fossils thought the dinosaur, a **plant-eater with three-foot-long claws,** (1-m) was a **giant turtle.**

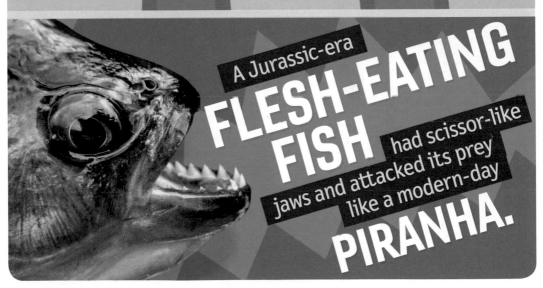

A Jurassic-era **FLESH-EATING FISH** had scissor-like jaws and attacked its prey like a modern-day **PIRANHA.**

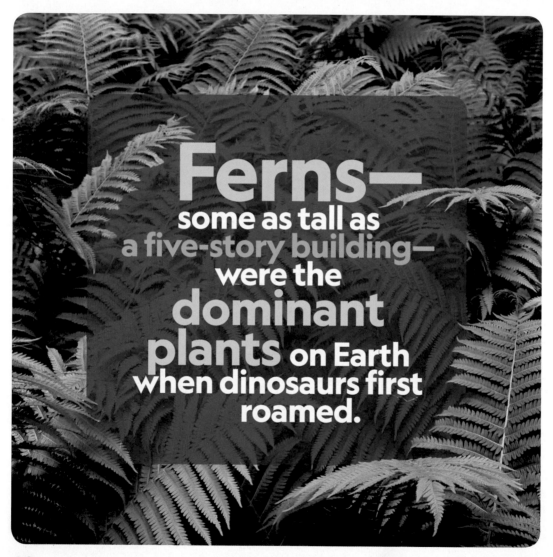

Ferns—
some as tall as
a five-story building—
were the
**dominant
plants** on Earth
when dinosaurs first
roamed.

A FLORIDA MAN HAS A COLLECTION OF **MORE THAN 1,200** PIECES OF **FOSSILIZED DINOSAUR POOP.**

Construction workers repairing a busy city street in China unearthed **43 dinosaur eggs.**

The skull of a *PENTACERATOPS* was longer than an NBA BASKETBALL PLAYER is tall.

The neck of **Elasmosaurus**, a marine reptile,

could grow to be as tall as a **two-story house.**

In 2007, a toy company made a full-size **baby *Triceratops*** toy that **kids could ride.**

Yutyrannus huali, **a giant theropod, was covered in fuzzy down** like a **baby chick.**

TRICERATOPS HAD

800

TEETH.

FLOSS
300 YDS.

In 2016, passengers on a flight from Chicago, Illinois, U.S.A., to the Netherlands flew with a **66-MILLION-YEAR-OLD *T. REX* FOSSIL** nicknamed Trix, who had **HER OWN PASSPORT.**

INTERNATIONAL PASSPORT

PASSPORT PASSEPORT

TYPE

CODE OF ISSUING STATE

PASSPORT NO.

SURNAME
Tyrannosaurus rex
GIVEN NAMES
Trix
NATIONALITY
Theropod
DATE OF BIRTH
66,398,000 years old
SEX
F

PLACE OF BIRTH
Montana

AUTHORITY

HOLDERS SIGNATURE

DATE OF ISSUE

DATE OF EXPIRY

WHEN TRIX ARRIVED, she was greeted with a caravan that included a **T. REX FLOAT AND A MARCHING BAND.**

You can buy a dinosaur-shaped TACO HOLDER.

Scutellosaurus had **armored plates** that were each smaller than a

bottle cap.

SOME DINOSAUR **SKULLS** WERE AS LONG AS A **REFRIGERATOR.**

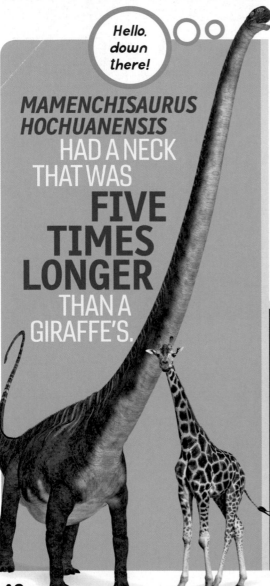

Hello, down there!

MAMENCHISAURUS HOCHUANENSIS HAD A NECK THAT WAS **FIVE TIMES LONGER** THAN A GIRAFFE'S.

One of the first *Allosaurus* fossils was mistaken for a petrified **horse hoof.**

THE LONG CLAWS OF *DEINOCHEIRUS MIRIFICUS* GAVE IT ITS NAME, WHICH MEANS **"UNUSUAL HORRIBLE HAND."**

Long-necked dinosaurs like *Apatosaurus* could live up to **100 years!**

Oh my...

Sea
turtles,
sharks,
horseshoe
crabs,
cockroaches,

platypuses, **and** **crocodiles** have all been around since the **time of the dinosaurs.**

THERE WERE **NO** *T. REX* IN SOUTH AMERICA.

SOME SCIENTISTS THINK THAT *GIGANOTOSAURUS* WEIGHED **10,000** POUNDS (4,535 kg) **MORE** THAN *TYRANNOSAURUS REX.*

Dinosaurs living near the **South Pole** had to **survive for months** in the dark.

Until scientists found the **BLUE-GREEN EGGS** of *Heyuannia huangi,* they thought all dinosaurs laid **WHITE EGGS.**

Velociraptor means "**speedy thief.**"

Tyrannosaurus means "**tyrant lizard.**"

"Dinosaur" means "terrible lizard."

Oviraptor means "egg stealer."

55

The first *Spinosaurus* bones, discovered in 1912, were **DESTROYED** in a **BOMBING RAID** on Munich, Germany, during World War II.

The first Carcharodontosaurus fossils were **BLOWN UP** by British bombers during the **SAME 1944 RAID.**

TRICERATOPS' HUGE HEAD MADE UP A THIRD OF ITS TOTAL BODY LENGTH.

Large fossilized mounds of **Ichthyosaur vomit** have been found in England.

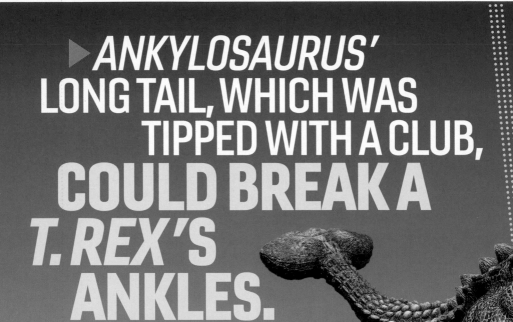

▶ *ANKYLOSAURUS'* LONG TAIL, WHICH WAS TIPPED WITH A CLUB, **COULD BREAK A** *T. REX'S* **ANKLES.**

▶ THE CLUB WAS AS BIG AS **TWO BASKETBALLS.**

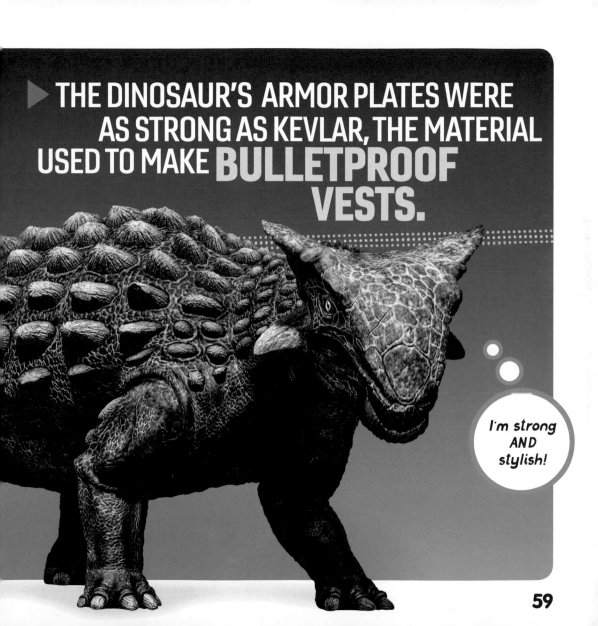

THE DINOSAUR'S ARMOR PLATES WERE AS STRONG AS KEVLAR, THE MATERIAL USED TO MAKE **BULLETPROOF VESTS.**

I'm strong AND stylish!

The **giant flying reptile,** *Quetzalcoatlus,* was as tall as a **giraffe** and may have **weighed** as much as a **tiger.**

With a **single, four-footed leap,** *Quetzalcoatlus* may have been able to **launch itself** into the air.

SAUROPODS ATE MORE THAN **1,000 POUNDS** (454 KG) OF **VEGETATION** A DAY.

At a **museum** in New Jersey, U.S.A., kids can visit a 15-foot (4.6-m)-long interactive **T. rex puppet.**

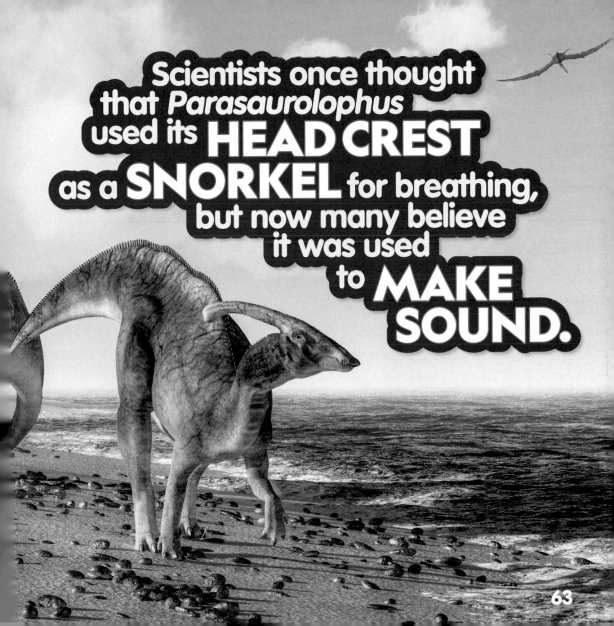

Scientists once thought that *Parasaurolophus* used its **HEAD CREST** as a **SNORKEL** for breathing, but now many believe it was used to **MAKE SOUND.**

TYRANNOSAURUS REX COULDN'T RUN— IT COULD ONLY WALK QUICKLY.

Some PLANT-EATING dinosaurs had CHEEK POUCHES like a chipmunk's so they could store food to EAT LATER.

The 48-foot (14.6-m)-long **Titanoboa,** the longest snake that ever lived, slithered through South America just after most dinosaurs became extinct.

Brachiosaurus may have **PASSED SO MUCH GAS** that they **WARMED EARTH'S OVERALL TEMPERATURE!**

Oops!

THE **LARGEST** DINOSAUR EGG EVER FOUND WAS AS LONG AS **ONE AND A HALF** FOOTBALLS.

A
**VOLCANIC
ERUPTION**
120 million years ago
BURIED A BIRD
so quickly that even
ITS LUNGS WERE
FOSSILIZED—
they were the first pair
EVER FOUND.

The
mascot
of the
Colorado
Rockies
baseball team is
Dinger,
a purple
Triceratops.

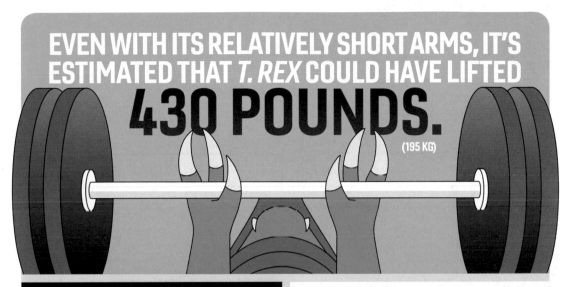

EVEN WITH ITS RELATIVELY SHORT ARMS, IT'S ESTIMATED THAT *T. REX* COULD HAVE LIFTED

430 POUNDS.

(195 KG)

Some dinosaurs may have **TRAVELED ACROSS A LAND BRIDGE** from Asia to North America more than **75 MILLION YEARS AGO.**

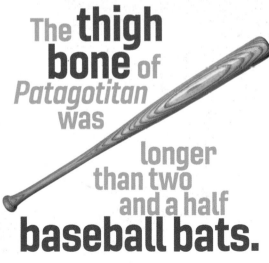

The **thigh bone** of *Patagotitan* was longer than two and a half **baseball bats.**

69

SARCOSUCHUS, a distant relative of modern crocodiles

that lived alongside dinosaurs, was AS LONG AS A BUS!

The one-and-a-half-foot-long (.46-m) **Micropachycephalosaurus** was one of the smallest dinosaurs— but has one of the longest names.

California, U.S.A., named *Augustynolophus morrisi,* a three-ton (2.7-t) member of the hadrosaur family, its official **state dinosaur.**

WELCOME TO
CALIFORNIA

At a hotel in Japan, **ROBOTIC DINOSAURS** worked the reception desk.

In 1982,
an eye doctor
suggested that
dinosaurs went
extinct because
**exposure to
the sun's rays**
made them
blind.

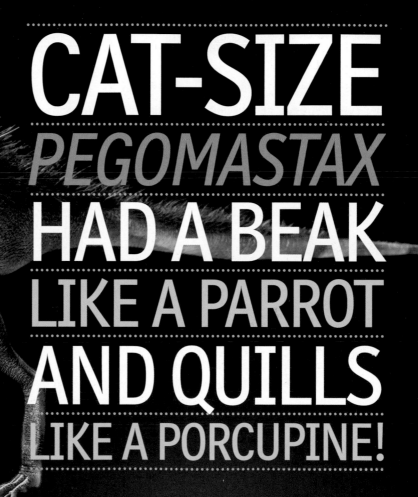

CAT-SIZE *PEGOMASTAX* HAD A BEAK LIKE A PARROT AND QUILLS LIKE A PORCUPINE!

Triceratops' teeth were SELF-SHARPENING.

The top of a *Pachycephalosaurus* skull was **nine inches** (23 cm) **thick—32 times thicker** than a **human's!**

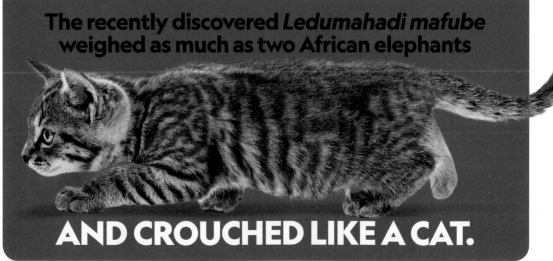

The recently discovered *Ledumahadi mafube* weighed as much as two African elephants

AND CROUCHED LIKE A CAT.

With a **DUCK-BILLED SNOUT** and a **SWANLIKE NECK,**

Halszkaraptor escuilliei **LOOKED SO ODD** that paleontologists thought it was **A MIX OF DIFFERENT FOSSILS.**

It was once believed that *Stegosaurus* had a **second brain in its back.**

Tyrannosaurus rex **COULD EASILY BITE THROUGH BONE.**

More than 2,000 years ago, fossilized **DINOSAUR BONES** found in China were identified as **DRAGON BONES.**

On the roller coaster **Flight of the Pterosaur** in the United Kingdom, riders soar over a re-created **prehistoric landscape.**

Like trees, DINOSAUR TEETH have growth lines that can be used to **ESTIMATE A DINOSAUR'S AGE.**

The character **Indiana Jones** was based in part on paleontologist Roy Chapman Andrews, who wore a **SIMILAR HAT** and also **HATED SNAKES.**

In 1991, paleontologist Paul Sereno **CRIED WITH JOY** when one of his team members discovered a perfectly preserved *Eoraptor* skull.

Some **floral scents** in popular perfumes have existed since the **time** of the **dinosaurs.**

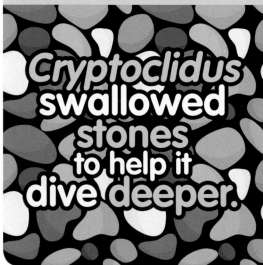

Cryptoclidus **swallowed stones** to help it **dive deeper.**

A family from Texas, U.S.A., **DRESSED UP AS *T. REX*** to announce that a **BABY WAS ON THE WAY.**

Quetzalcoatlus, a flying reptile with a **35-foot** (11-m) wingspan,

likely ate baby dinosaurs.

**CANADA MINTED
A GLOW-IN-THE-DARK
25-CENT COIN**
FEATURING
*PACHYRHINOSAURUS
LAKUSTAI.*

A restaurant in Brandon, Manitoba, Canada, once sold a **nine-patty** *"T. rex burger"* for **$21.99.**

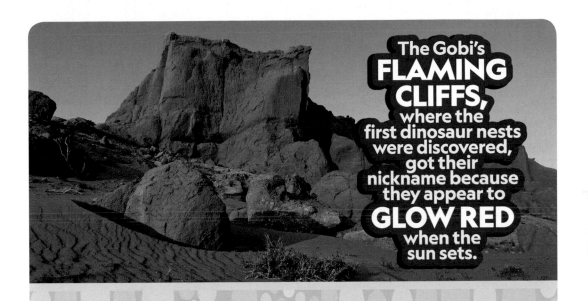

The Gobi's **FLAMING CLIFFS,** where the first dinosaur nests were discovered, got their nickname because they appear to **GLOW RED** when the sun sets.

Egg Mountain, IN MONTANA, U.S.A., WAS NAMED FOR THE **14 dinosaur nests** FOUND THERE.

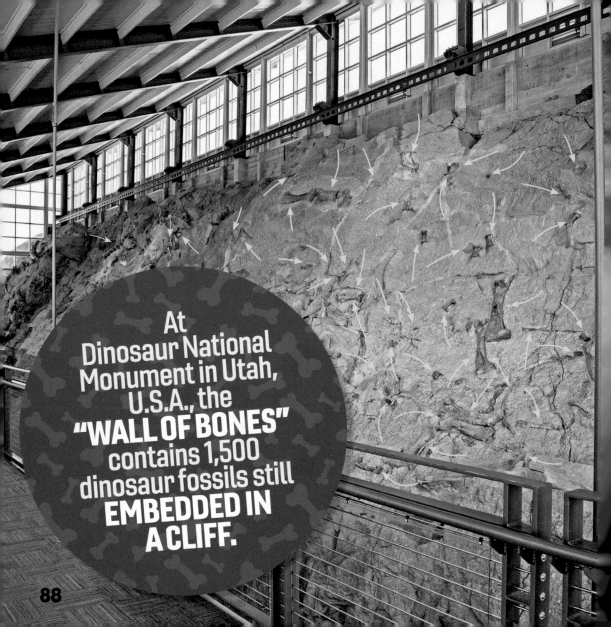

At Dinosaur National Monument in Utah, U.S.A., the **"WALL OF BONES"** contains 1,500 dinosaur fossils still **EMBEDDED IN A CLIFF.**

A PILE OF 130-MILLION-YEAR-OLD FOSSILIZED DINOSAUR POOP SOLD AT AN AUCTION FOR $960.

SOLD

DINOSAUR FAIRYLAND, in Inner Mongolia, China, has DOZENS of LIFE-SIZE DINO MODELS, but it's so remote that few people visit.

Amargasaurus had spines on its neck that were twice as long as a dinner knife.

When it **shook,** the spines **clattered—** to sound a **warning,** one scientist thinks.

In the small town of **Dinosaur, Colorado, U.S.A.,** you can live on

TRICERATOPS TERRACE,

DIPLODOCUS DRIVE, OR

BRACHIOSAURUS STREET.

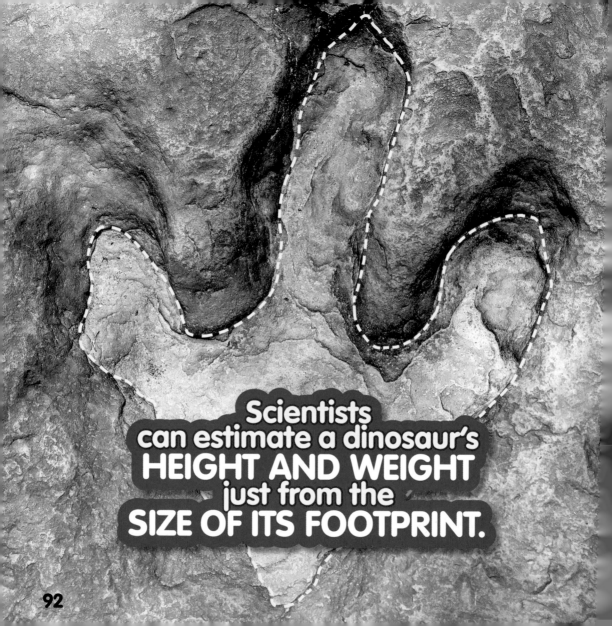

Scientists can estimate a dinosaur's **HEIGHT AND WEIGHT** just from the **SIZE OF ITS FOOTPRINT.**

Pterosaurs
FLEW LIKE BIRDS BUT WALKED ON ALL FOURS,
using their wing hands for balance.

T. REX was more **CLOSELY RELATED** to **SPARROWS** than to **TRICERATOPS.**

SAUROPOD TRACKS
FOUND ON SCOTLAND'S ISLE OF SKYE

ARE AS **WIDE AS A CAR TIRE.**

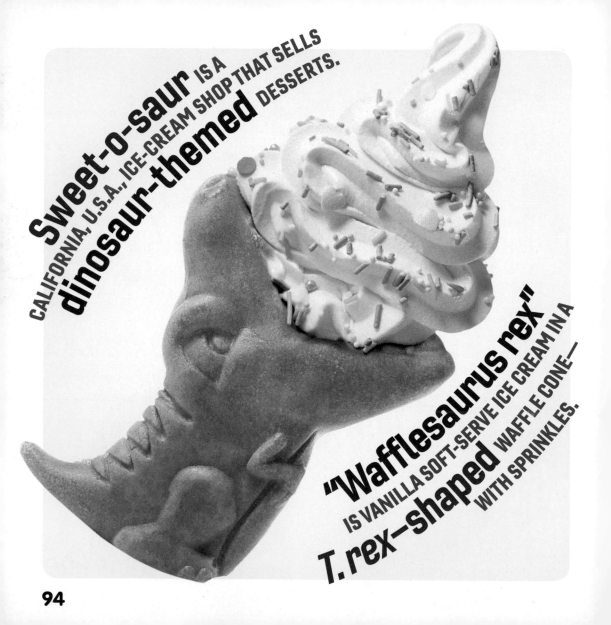

Sweet-o-saur IS A CALIFORNIA, U.S.A., ICE-CREAM SHOP THAT SELLS **dinosaur-themed** DESSERTS.

"**Wafflesaurus rex**" IS VANILLA SOFT-SERVE ICE CREAM IN A **T. rex–shaped** WAFFLE CONE— WITH SPRINKLES.

One kind of tyrannosaur with a **LONG, SLENDER SNOUT** is nicknamed **PINOCCHIO REX.**

Researchers study FOSSILIZED DINOSAUR POOP to figure out WHAT DINOSAURS ATE.

The asteroid that killed most of Earth's dinosaurs **66 million years ago** left a crater **larger than Vermont,** U.S.A.

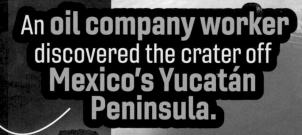

An **oil company worker** discovered the crater off **Mexico's Yucatán Peninsula.**

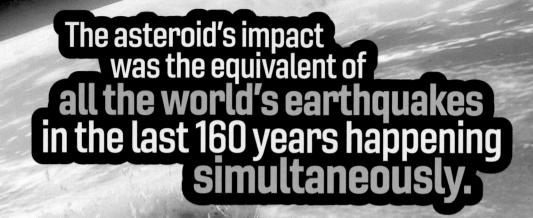

The asteroid's impact was the equivalent of **all the world's earthquakes in the last 160 years happening simultaneously.**

Sauropods, **the largest animals to ever walk the Earth, had a brain the size of a tennis ball.**

Air-filled pockets in their vertebrae helped lighten **their weight.**

You can **TAKE A SHOWER** underneath a five-inch (13-cm)-tall *TYRANNOSAURUS* HEAD.

Some dinosaurs had **RETRACTABLE CLAWS** like cats' claws.

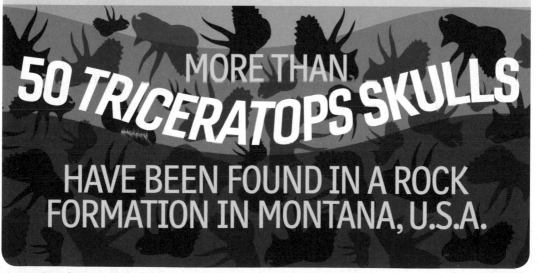

MORE THAN **50 TRICERATOPS SKULLS** HAVE BEEN FOUND IN A ROCK FORMATION IN MONTANA, U.S.A.

A DINOSAUR-ERA **SNAIL** FOSSILIZED IN AMBER CONTAINS A PRESERVED **SHELL** AND **HEAD** TENTACLE.

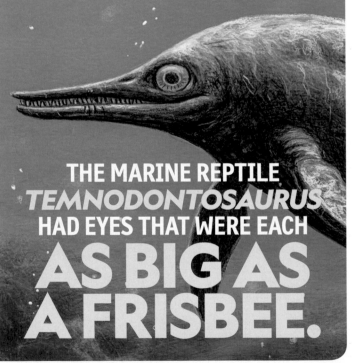

HUMANS ARE **CLOSER IN TIME** TO THE **LAST *T. REX*** THAN *T. REX* WAS TO *STEGOSAURUS*.

THE MARINE REPTILE ***TEMNODONTOSAURUS*** HAD EYES THAT WERE EACH **AS BIG AS A FRISBEE.**

IT TOOK A DINOSAUR EGG UP TO **SIX MONTHS** TO HATCH!

It takes an ostrich egg **ONLY 42 DAYS.**

An **AMMONITE**, a marine animal from the Jurassic and Cretaceous, moved by **SQUIRTING JETS** of water from its body.

Psittacosaurus had **horns** on its **cheeks.**

A FOSSILIZED *BARYONX* INCLUDED PARTIALLY DIGESTED **FISH SCALES** IN ITS STOMACH.

The ancestors of Chinese **giant salamanders**

Hi, buddy!

lived among **dinosaurs.**

MAIASAURA may have migrated back to their **BIRTHPLACE** to **LAY EGGS**—like **SEA TURTLES** do today.

With its "bandit mask" eyes and a striped tail, *Sinosauropteryx* looked like a **LONG RACCOON.**

Giant flealike insects, about 10 times larger than fleas today, fed on the **blood** of **dinosaurs.**

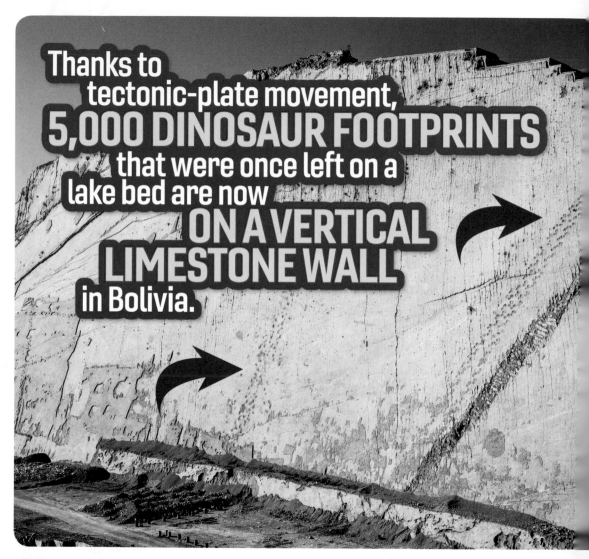

Thanks to tectonic-plate movement, **5,000 DINOSAUR FOOTPRINTS** that were once left on a lake bed are now **ON A VERTICAL LIMESTONE WALL** in Bolivia.

THE EARLIEST KNOWN DINOSAURS WERE ONLY ABOUT **THE SIZE** OF TODAY'S **LABRADOR RETRIEVERS.**

Just by clicking the **space bar,** you can move a **dinosaur** in a **Google game.**

THE 2016 MACY'S THANKSGIVING DAY PARADE IN NEW YORK CITY FEATURED

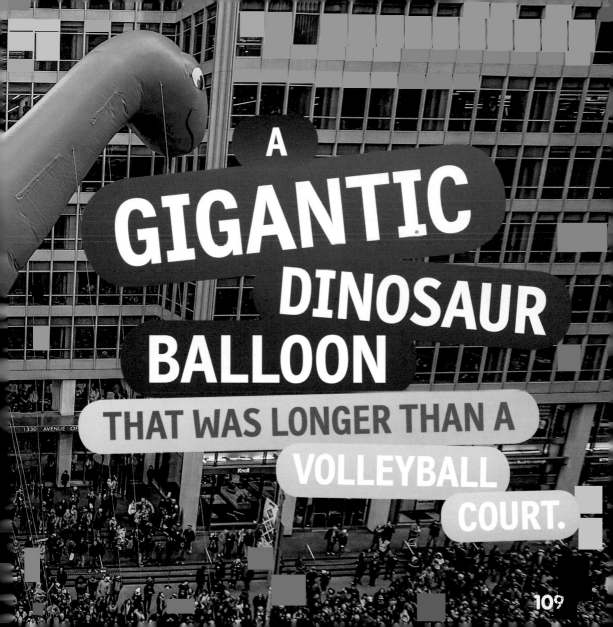

A **GIGANTIC DINOSAUR BALLOON** THAT WAS LONGER THAN A VOLLEYBALL COURT.

Cryolophosaurus was nicknamed **Elvisaurus** for its Elvis-like "hair"—a curved crest atop its head.

I've got a rockin' dino 'do.

A new dinosaur species is discovered **almost every week.**

Dino discovery!

SOME DINOSAURS MAY HAVE USED "BABYSITTERS" TO WATCH OVER THEIR HATCHLINGS.

Spinosaurus is the **LARGEST KNOWN PREDATORY DINOSAUR—** it was nine feet (2.7 m) longer than *T. REX!*

One man made a **20-FOOT-LONG** (6-m) *T. rex* from **80,020** LEGO BRICKS.

Theropod tracks in Inner Mongolia, China, inspired local farmers to imagine they were left by a **divine bird.**

The *MEI LONG* dinosaur slept with its **head tucked,** just like **TODAY'S BIRDS** sleep.

Researchers can tell if a dinosaur was **nocturnal** based on the shape of its **eye sockets.**

Some scientists believe that if an asteroid hadn't **HIT EARTH** 66 million years ago, some extinct dinosaurs would be **LIVING TODAY.**

You can buy a **TRICERATOPS COSTUME,** including a head frill and horns, **FOR YOUR DOG OR CAT.**

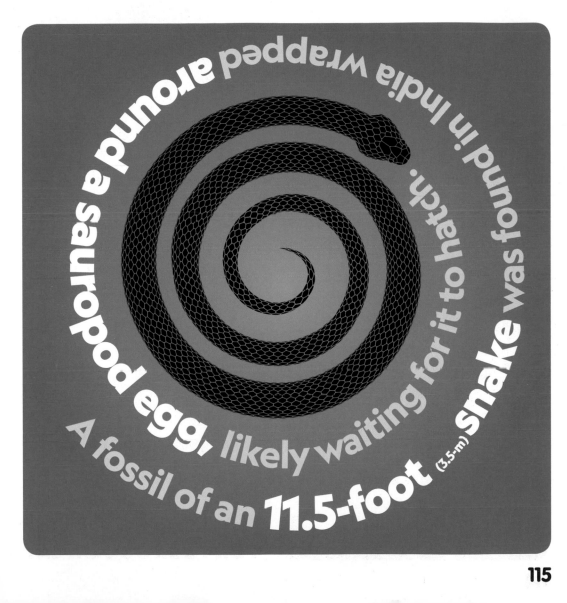

A fossil of an **11.5-foot** (3.5-m) **snake** was found in India wrapped around a sauropod egg, likely waiting for it to hatch.

If alive today, **BRACHIOSAURUS** could snack on **PLANTS** growing in a **FOURTH-STORY WINDOW BOX.**

During the Late Cretaceous, just before most dinosaurs went extinct, much of North America was **COVERED IN SHALLOW WATER.**

PTEROSAURS, flying reptiles that lived **200 MILLION YEARS AGO,** may have had a pouch **LIKE A PELICAN.**

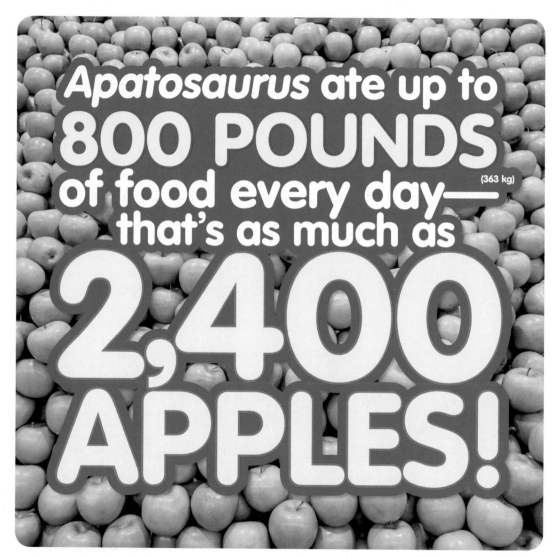

Apatosaurus ate up to **800 POUNDS** of food every day— (363 kg) that's as much as **2,400 APPLES!**

Pachycephalosaurus may have used its **nine-inch** (23-cm)- **thick skull** for **head-butting.**

MICRORAPTOR WEIGHED LESS THAN A **PINT** (0.5 L) OF **MILK.**

Tyrannosaurus rex may have **hunted in packs.**

A full-grown 105-foot (32-m)-long *Diplodocus* **was probably too big to be hunted by any predators.**

As the supercontinent Pangaea broke apart, Great Britain provided a land bridge between Eurasia and North America for dinosaurs to travel across.

MICRORAPTORS HAD **LONG FEATHERS** ON FOUR LIMBS BUT **COULDN'T FLY—** THEY COULD ONLY **GLIDE DOWN** FROM TREETOPS.

There is a **121-foot** (37-m) **hot-air balloon** shaped like a **T. rex.**

SOME **ICHTHYOSAURS**— AQUATIC REPTILES THAT LIVED WITH THE DINOSAURS— GREW TO BE ABOUT THE SIZE OF **BLUE WHALES.**

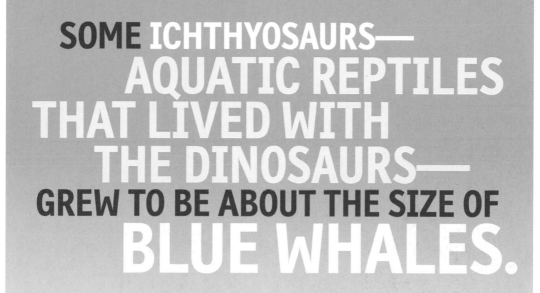

A paleontologist **stranded in a field** by a flat tire found the fossil remains of **"Sue,"** the most complete *Tyrannosaurus rex* skeleton ever discovered.

SCIENTISTS THINK THAT **SOME DINOSAUR EGGS WERE COLORED** TO **CAMOUFLAGE THEM IN THEIR NESTS.**

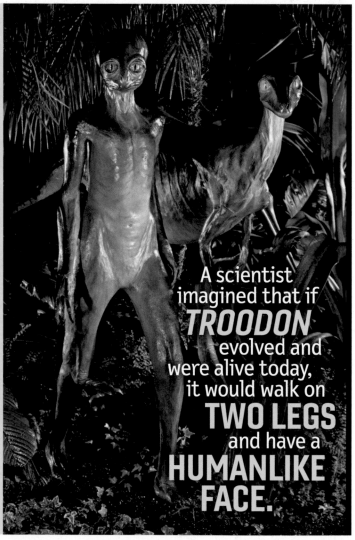

A scientist imagined that if *TROODON* evolved and were alive today, it would walk on **TWO LEGS** and have a **HUMANLIKE FACE.**

The **head frill** on a *Triceratops* was as wide as a **car.**

HELLO
MY NAME IS
Megalosaurus

Megalosaurus WAS THE **FIRST DINOSAUR** EVER NAMED— NEARLY 200 YEARS AGO.

The supercontinent **PANGAEA** had few tall mountains—it was

MOSTLY FLAT.

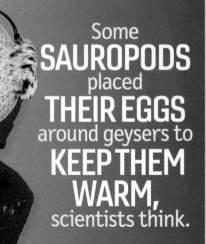

Some **SAUROPODS** placed **THEIR EGGS** around geysers to **KEEP THEM WARM,** scientists think.

In 2007, a collector **bought a mosasaur fossil** for more than $350,000.

A DINOSAUR MUSEUM
ON ENGLAND'S
ISLE OF WIGHT

WAS BUILT TO LOOK LIKE A
PTEROSAUR.

GIFTSHOP
& WINTER

Brachiosaurus's **NOSTRILS** were on the **TOP OF ITS HEAD.**

TYRANNOSAURUS REX'S **VISION** WAS **13 TIMES SHARPER** THAN A HUMAN'S.

Some early mammals that lived with the dinosaurs were about the size of a bumblebee.

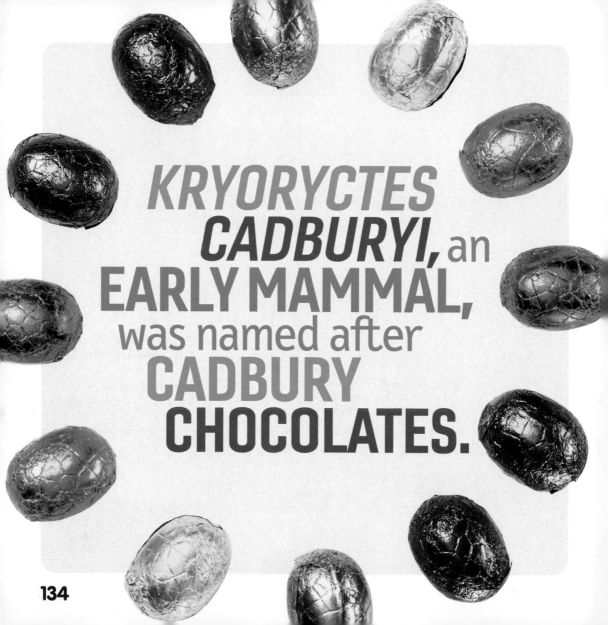

KRYORYCTES CADBURYI, an **EARLY MAMMAL,** was named after **CADBURY CHOCOLATES.**

One scientist thought that *Archaeopteryx*, considered to be the **THE FIRST BIRD,** was a **FAKE FOSSIL.**

In the 1980s animated TV show *DINOSAUCERS,* dinosaurs lived on a **TWIN PLANET EARTH** that wasn't hit by an asteroid, and they drove around in **DINOSAUR-SHAPED SPACESHIPS.**

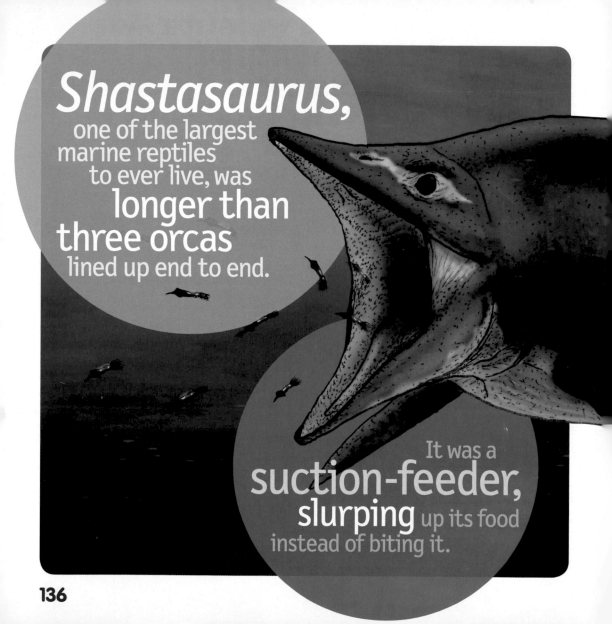

Shastasaurus, one of the largest marine reptiles to ever live, was **longer than three orcas** lined up end to end.

It was a **suction-feeder, slurping** up its food instead of biting it.

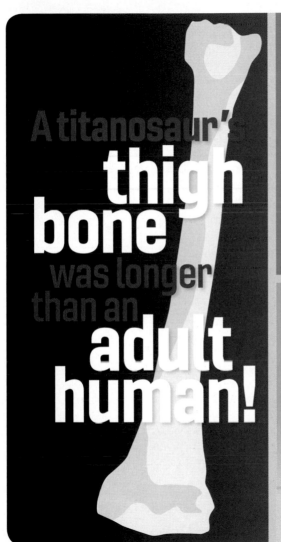

A titanosaur's **thigh bone** was longer than an **adult human!**

T. REX COULDN'T STICK OUT ITS **TONGUE.**

Birdlike oviraptorids may have **CUDDLED TOGETHER** when they slept.

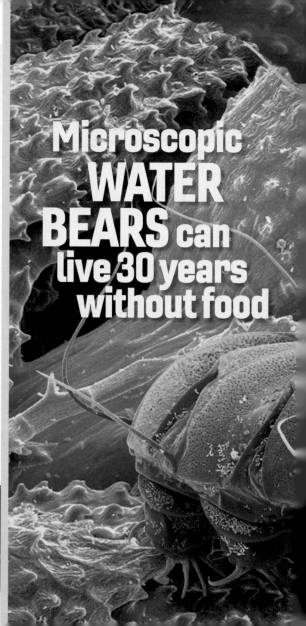

Microscopic **WATER BEARS** can live 30 years without food

A South Korean dessert shop sells a
chocolate egg
that diners hit with a
small hammer

to reveal a
dinosaur
inside.

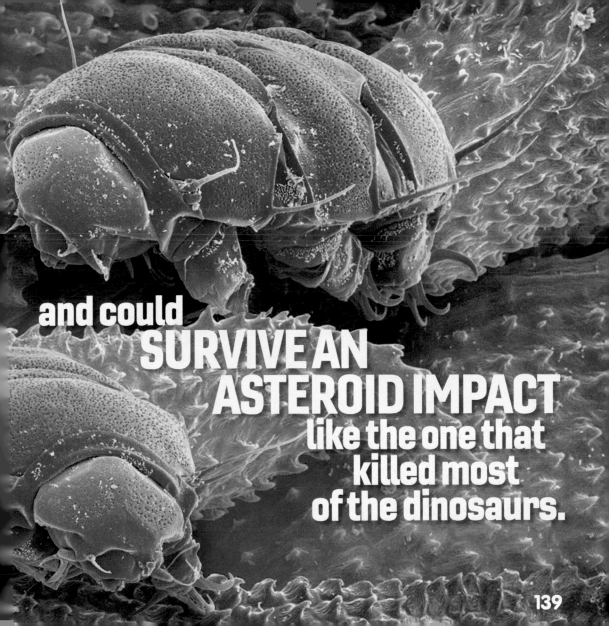

and could **SURVIVE AN ASTEROID IMPACT** like the one that killed most of the dinosaurs.

T. rex likely held its hands in a **clapping position,** a new study found.

Heterodontosaurus's PINKIE was on BACKWARD.

Some dinosaurs **swallowed stones** to help them digest **their food.**

London's Natural History Museum stored a *Diplodocus* fossil cast

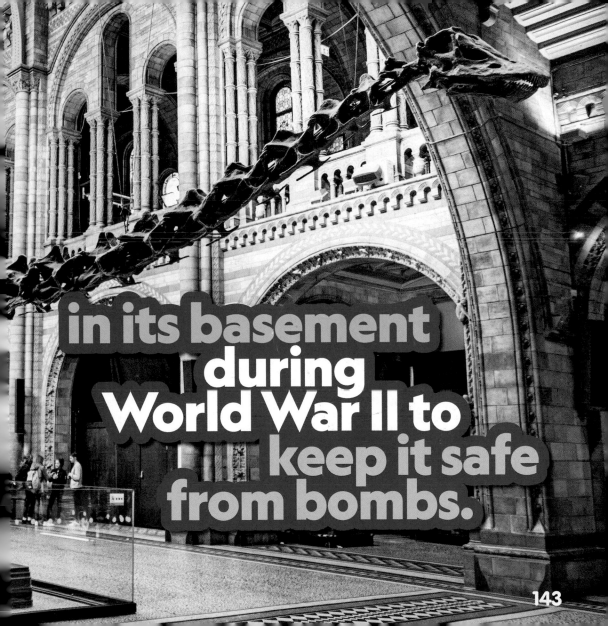

in its basement during World War II to keep it safe from bombs.

143

A Canadian man made a **LIFE-SIZE** *TYRANNOSAURUS REX* out of more than **600 BALLOONS.**

ARGENTINOSAURUS,

the longest dinosaur ever found, was
LONGER THAN AN NBA BASKETBALL COURT—
over 130 feet
(40 m) long.

Quicksand
has been
around since
**THE TIME OF
THE DINOSAURS.**

SPINOSAURUS
SNACKED ON
SHARKS.

Yikes!

SCIENTISTS FOUND A HOLE IN AN *ALLOSAURUS* FOSSIL, POSSIBLY CAUSED BY A *STEGOSAURUS* TAIL SPIKE.

Urolites
are preserved holes
in the ground where
dinosaurs peed.

Who you gonna call?

Zuul crurivastator
was named after the demon in
Ghostbusters.

More than **40 life-size dinosaurs** stretch along a 1.5-mile (2.4-km)-long footpath in Oakdale, Connecticut, U.S.A.

To enter the Ancient Times restaurant in Yamato, Japan, diners walk **THROUGH A GIGANTIC T. REX MOUTH** and eat alongside 20 **ANIMATRONIC** dinosaurs.

A man DRESSED AS A DINOSAUR ran the LONDON MARATHON in less than three hours and nine minutes.

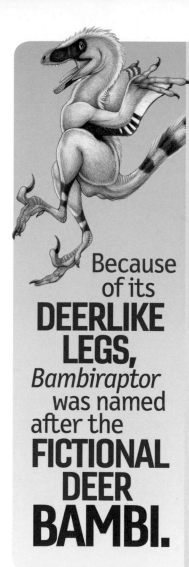

Because of its **DEERLIKE LEGS,** *Bambiraptor* was named after the **FICTIONAL DEER BAMBI.**

A NEARLY **COMPLETE FOSSIL** OF A *PSITTACOSAURUS* ALLOWED SCIENTISTS TO IDENTIFY THE DINOSAUR'S **SKIN COLORS.**

Researchers think some dinosaurs got **so big** because they used **energy for growing** instead of keeping their bodies warm.

A *T. rex*'s bite was **10 TIMES MORE FORCEFUL** than a **modern alligator's.**

Beibeilong sinensis, a birdlike dinosaur, laid eggs as big as beach balls.

Scientists think **PLATEOSAURUS** **FOSSILS ARE SO PLENTIFUL** because these dinosaurs **GOT STUCK IN THE MUD** while trying to eat plants.

During HALFTIME at a college football game in Iowa, U.S.A., a troupe of **TYRANNOSAURS DANCED** while the band played THE *JURASSIC PARK* THEME SONG.

DIPPY THE DINOSAUR, a life-size statue of a ***DIPLODOCUS CARNEGII*** outside a museum in Pittsburgh, Pennsylvania, U.S.A., has its own **SOCIAL MEDIA ACCOUNT.**

DEINONYCHUS had a sickle-shaped **TOE CLAW** that it could flick like a knife to **SLASH THROUGH FLESH.**

You can buy **Popsicle molds** shaped like dinosaurs.

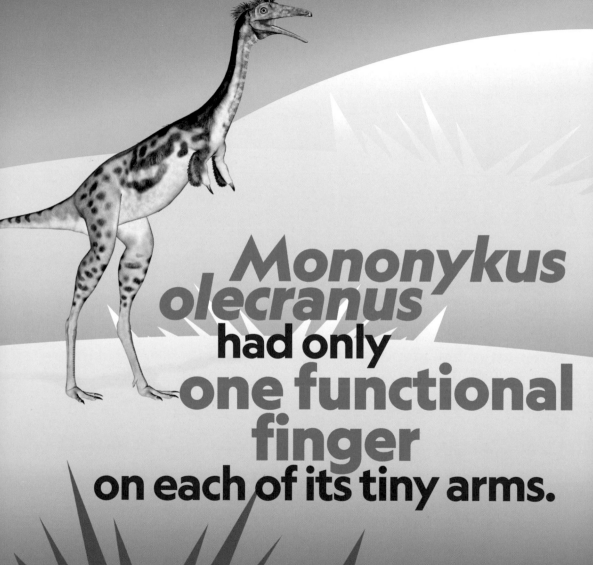

Mononykus olecranus had only **one functional finger** on each of its tiny arms.

It may have used its finger to **dig into ant nests,** like today's **anteaters do.**

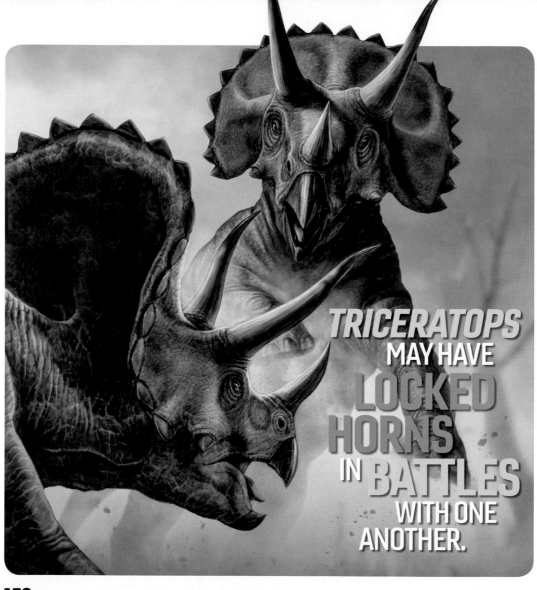

TRICERATOPS MAY HAVE **LOCKED HORNS** IN **BATTLES** WITH ONE ANOTHER.

IN 2018, A 150-MILLION-YEAR-OLD DINOSAUR FOSSIL WAS SOLD AT AN AUCTION FOR $2.36 MILLION.

Dinosaurs may have been stung by early kinds of bees.

Mary Anning, considered one of the world's greatest **fossil hunters,** made a living in the early 19th century **finding and selling fossils.**

YOU CAN BUY **JEWELRY** MADE OF

FOSSILIZED DINOSAUR **POOP.**

Meat-eating dinosaurs laid **LONG AND THIN EGGS,** while plant-eating dinosaurs laid **ROUNDER EGGS.**

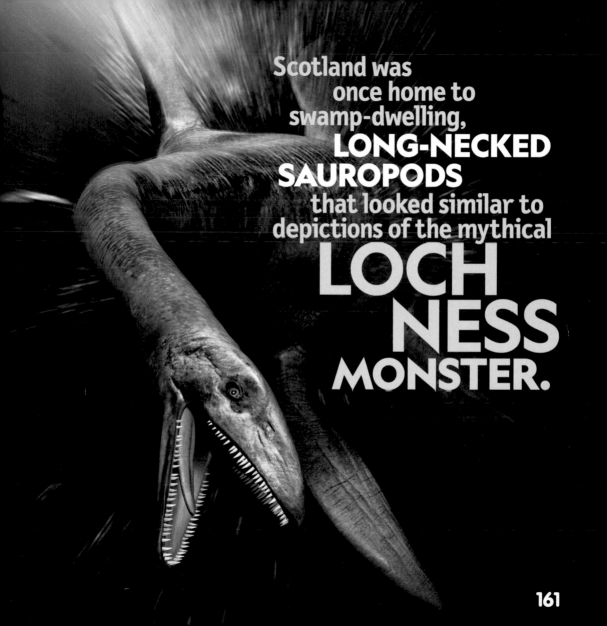

Scotland was once home to swamp-dwelling, **LONG-NECKED SAUROPODS** that looked similar to depictions of the mythical **LOCH NESS MONSTER.**

The gigantic **Dinny the *Apatosaurus*** in Cabazon, California, U.S.A., took about **10 years to build.**

During the Jurassic, temperatures in  may have never dipped below freezing; today, winter temperatures of **-60°F** (-51°C) **are** considered normal there.

In a poll that asked Americans what **EXOTIC ANIMAL** they'd like as **A PET,** **18 PERCENT SAID** **A DINOSAUR.**

THE CLOSEST
LIVING
RELATIVES OF

T.REX
ARE
CHICKENS
AND
OSTRICHES.

UTAHRAPTOR'S
NINE-INCH-
(23-CM)
LONG CLAW
WAS MORE THAN
TWICE
AS LONG
AS A TIGER'S.

AN ADULT *DIPLODOCUS* GOT A

NEW TOOTH
EVERY
35 DAYS.

Troodontids are considered to have been one of the **smartest** dinosaurs.

Euoplocephalus tutus had
ARMORED EYELIDS:
Bony plates could slide over its eyes for protection.

SELF-TAUGHT **FOSSIL HUNTER** Ray Stanford has found **HUNDREDS OF DINOSAUR TRACKS** NEAR HIS HOME in the Washington, D.C., U.S.A., area.

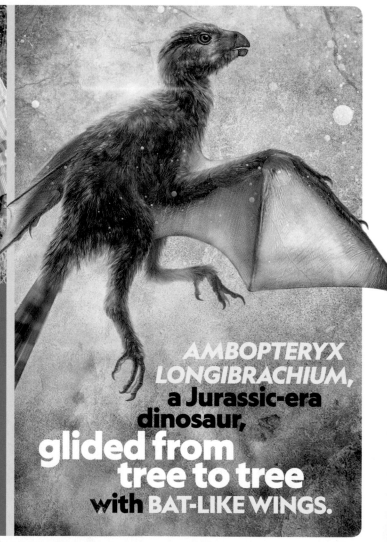

AMBOPTERYX LONGIBRACHIUM, a Jurassic-era dinosaur, **glided from tree to tree** with BAT-LIKE WINGS.

PACHYCEPHALOSAURUS'S
TEETH WERE SMALLER
THAN A HUMAN
TODDLER'S TEETH.

SOME DINOSAURS MIGHT HAVE **DANCED** TO **IMPRESS** THEIR MATES.

It can take **SCIENTISTS DECADES** to understand **NEW FOSSIL FINDS.**

At the **T-REX CAFE** in Florida, U.S.A., you'll find a dino-themed menu, life-size **ANIMATRONIC DINOSAURS,** and a play area with a fossil sandpit.

Mussaurus means **"mouse lizard"** because scientists thought the babies were **full-grown** adults.

Rawr!

Scientists are **STUDYING PARROTS** to see if some dinosaurs **HOPPED** when trying to fly.

In 2006, a dinosaur hunter found the fossils of two "DUELING" DINOSAURS— a huge horned dinosaur LOCKED IN COMBAT with a smaller tyrannosaur.

A Texas, U.S.A., family built a drivable **"hippysaurus"** for an **art-car parade.**

In remote places, paleontologists use drones to spot dinosaur tracks.

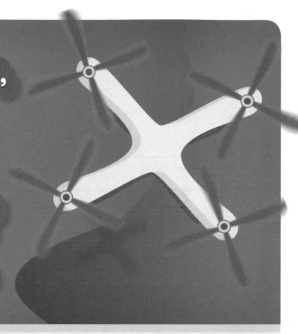

OOSPECIES
= A DINOSAUR KNOWN ONLY FROM ITS EGGS

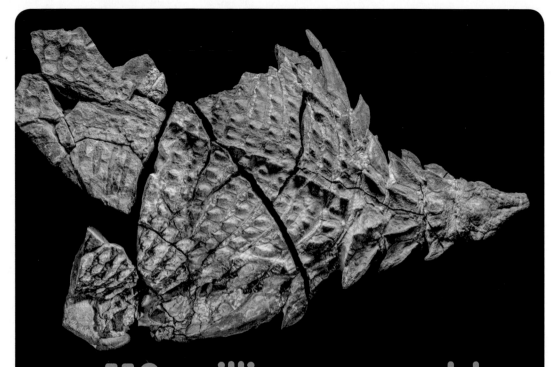

A **110-million-year-old** nodosaur fossil from **western Canada** was so **WELL PRESERVED** that its **STOMACH** still had **remnants** of its **last meal.**

BIRDS ARE DINOSAURS.

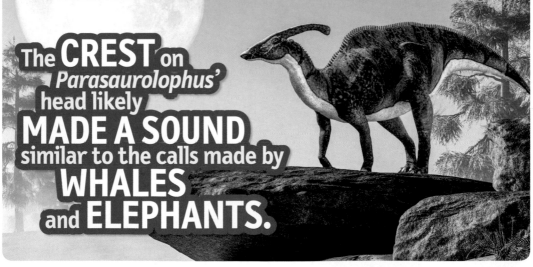

The **CREST** on *Parasaurolophus'* head likely **MADE A SOUND** similar to the calls made by **WHALES** and **ELEPHANTS.**

Scientists once thought that **sauropods lived in the sea,** sticking their long necks out of the water to breathe.

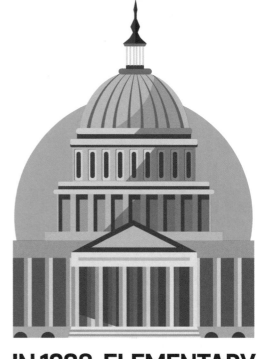

IN 1998, ELEMENTARY SCHOOL STUDENTS NAMED A DINOSAUR FOSSIL FOUND IN WASHINGTON, D.C., U.S.A., CAPITALSAURUS.

Psittacosaurus, an early horned dinosaur, may have had **colored quills on its tail,** used for **showing off** to other dinosaurs.

SOUTH KOREA'S GONGRYONG RIDGE IS THOUGHT TO RESEMBLE A **DINOSAUR SPINE.**

179

GOOGLE headquarters in California, U.S.A., has a **FULL-SIZE** *T. REX* replica named **STAN.**

Stegosaurus, or **"ROOFED LIZARD,"** was named for the way the plates on its back lay flat, **LIKE SHINGLES ON A ROOF.**

IN 1985, NASA SENT A MAIASAURA **BONE FRAGMENT** AND PARTIAL EGGSHELL ON **A MISSION INTO SPACE.**

THE WORLD'S **OLDEST DANDRUFF** WAS FOUND FOSSILIZED ON A 125-MILLION-YEAR-OLD, FOUR-WINGED *MICRORAPTOR.*

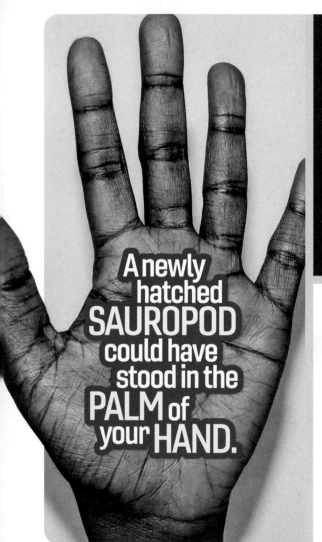

A newly hatched **SAUROPOD** could have stood in the **PALM** of your **HAND.**

WHISKER-LIKE FACE FEATHERS HELPED SOME DINOSAURS MAKE **MORE PRECISE** ATTACKS ON PREY.

In South Dakota, U.S.A., you can see a metal sculpture of a **human skeleton walking a T. rex skeleton** on a leash.

YOU CAN BUY A PRADA *STEGOSAURUS-*THEMED BAG FOR ABOUT **$3,000.**

Who, me?

Carnotaurus had **devilish horns** on its head.

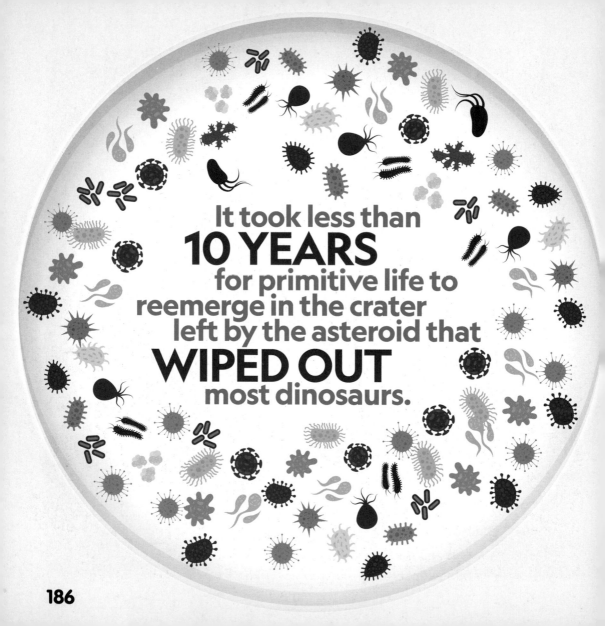

It took less than
10 YEARS
for primitive life to
reemerge in the crater
left by the asteroid that
WIPED OUT
most dinosaurs.

THE FIRST LARGE **DINOSAUR PARK—** CRYSTAL PALACE PARK IN LONDON, ENGLAND— IS MORE THAN **165 YEARS OLD.**

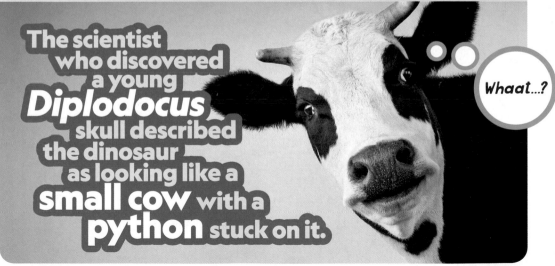

The scientist who discovered a young *Diplodocus* skull described the dinosaur as looking like a **small cow** with a **python** stuck on it.

Whaat...?

IN THE UNITED STATES, IF YOU FIND A DINOSAUR FOSSIL IN YOUR BACKYARD, YOU CAN KEEP IT.

The **YOUNGEST** person to **find a fossil** of an **unknown dinosaur** species was a **SEVEN-YEAR-OLD** boy from Chile.

Some dinosaurs had **1,000 teeth.**

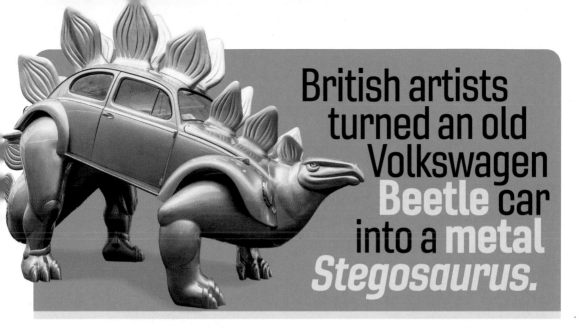

British artists turned an old Volkswagen **Beetle** car into a **metal** *Stegosaurus.*

A TEXAS STORE SELLS A **16-FOOT-TALL**(5-M) CONCRETE *BRACHIOSAURUS* THAT GOES FOR ALMOST **$12,000.**

Araucaria trees, which *Argentinosaurus*— the world's heaviest dinosaur—ate, **still grow** in Argentina.

A **99-MILLION-YEAR-OLD FEATHERED DINOSAUR** tail was recently found in a **PIECE OF AMBER.**

DRACOREX HOGWARTSIA got its name from **HOGWARTS SCHOOL** in the Harry Potter series.

SCIENTISTS THOUGHT THAT **COELACANTHS,** A TYPE OF FISH, **DIED OFF** WITH THE DINOSAURS— UNTIL **A LIVING ONE** WAS SPOTTED IN 1938.

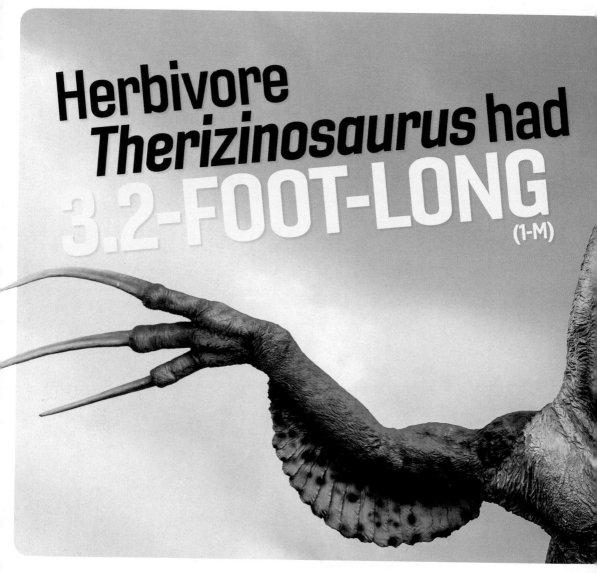

Herbivore
Therizinosaurus had
3.2-FOOT-LONG
(1-M)

CLAWS—
the longest of any dinosaur.

The **OLDEST MAMMAL** discovered in Brazil, *BRASILESTES STARDUSTI,* is named after David Bowie's character **ZIGGY STARDUST.**

All we know about this creature comes from just **ONE TOOTH.**

A **beagle** discovered a 250,000-year-old **woolly rhino bone.**

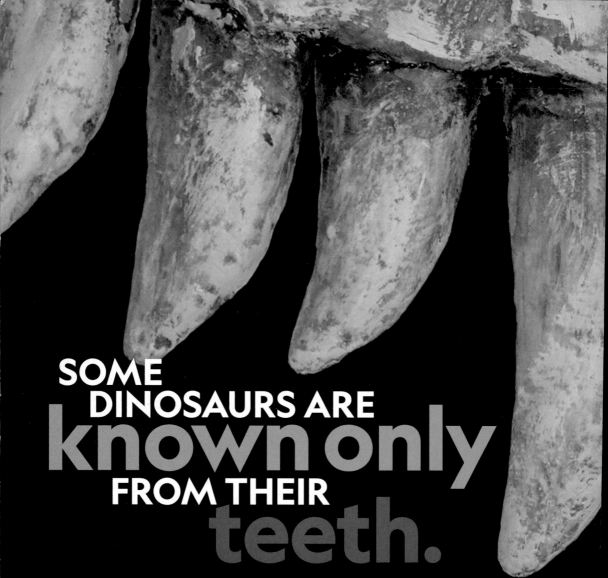

SOME DINOSAURS ARE known only FROM THEIR teeth.

PRONUNCIATION GUIDE

Allosaurus
AL-oh-SORE-us

Amargasaurus
uh-MARG-uh-SORE-us

Ankylosaurus
AN-kye-loh-SORE-us

Apatosaurus
uh-PAT-uh-SORE-us

Archaeopteryx
ARK-ee-OP-turr-icks

Argentinosaurus
ahr-gen-TEEN-oh-SORE-us

Augustynolophus morrisi
awe-GUS-TEEN-oh-loh-fuss
more-iss-ee

Bambiraptor
BAM-be-RAP-tore

Baryonx
BARE-ee-ON-icks

Beibeilong sinensis
bay-bay-long sih-nen-sis

Brachiosaurus
BRACK-ee-oh-SORE-us

Brasilestes stardusti
bra-ZIL-es-tees star-dust-ee

Caihong juji
KAY-hong ju-gee

Capitalsaurus
CAP-e-tall-SORE-us

Carcharodontosaurus
CAR-care-oh-DON-toe-SORE-us

Carnotaurus
KAR-no-TORE-us

Cretalamna bryanti
KREH-ta-lom-na bri-ON-tee

Cryolophosaurus
CRY-oh-LOW-fo-SORE-us

Cryptoclidus
KRIP-ta-KLID-us

Deinocheirus mirificus
DINE-oh-KYE-russ
meer-IF-ee-kus

Deinonychus
die-NON-e-kuss

Diplodocus carnegii
dih-PLOD-uh-kus car-NIH-gee

Dracorex hogwartsia
DRAY-co-rex hog-WART-see-ah

Edmontosaurus
ed-MON-toh-SORE-us

Elasmosaurus
EE-laz-mo-SORE-us

Eoraptor
EE-oh-RAP-tore

Euoplocephalus tutus
YOU-oh-plo-SEF-ah-lus
TOO-toos

Gastonia
gas-TONE-ee-ah

Giganotosaurus
JEYE-ga-NO-toe-SORE-us

Halszkaraptor escuilliei
halz-ka-RAP-tore
es-KWEE-lee-a

Heterodontosaurus
HET-er-oh-DON-toe-SORE-us

Heyuannia huangi
HEY-yoo-on-nee-ya WONG-ee

Kosmoceratops
COZ-mo-SERR-ah-tops

Kryoryctes cadburyi
cry-oh-RICK-tees cad-BURR-ee

Ledumahadi mafube
la-DOOM-ah-hodd-ee
ma-FOO-bee

Maiasaura
MA-ya-SORE-a

Mamenchisaurus hochuanensis
mah-MEHN-chee-SORE-us ho-CHOO-an-EN-sis

Megalosaurus
MEG-ah-low-SORE-us

Mei long
MAY-long

Micropachycephalosaurus
MY-crow-pack-ih-SEF-ah-low-SORE-us

Microraptor
MY-crow-RAP-tore

Mononykus olecranus
mon-NO-nih-cuss oh-LEC-ran-us

Mussaurus
moo-SORE-us

Oviraptor
OH-vih-RAP-tore

Pachycephalosaurus
pack-ih-SEF-ah-low-SORE-us

Pachyrhinosaurus lakustai
pack-ee-RINE-oh-SORE-us la-KOOS-tie

Parasaurolophus
PAR-ah-saw-RAH-loh-fuss

Patagotitan mayorum
PAT-a-go-TIE-tan MAY-or-umm

Pegomastax
peg-oh-MASS-tacks

Pentaceratops
PEN-ta-SER-ah-tops

Plateosaurus
PLAT-ee-oh-SORE-us

Psittacosaurus
SIT-ah-co-SORE-us

Quetzalcoatlus
ket-zall-co-AT-lus

Sarcosuchus
SAHR-co-SOOCH-us

Scutellosaurus
skoo-TELL-oh-SORE-us

Shastasaurus
shas-ta-SORE-us

Sinosauropteryx
SINE-oh-sore-OP-ter-iks

Spinosaurus
SPINE-oh-SORE-us

Stegosaurus
STEG-oh-SORE-us

Temnodontosaurus
TIM-no-DON-toe-SORE-us

Therizinosaurus
THERE-ih-ZIN-oh-SORE-us

Titanoboa
TIE-tan-oh-bow-ah

Titanosaur
TIE-tan-oh-SORE

Tratayenia rosalesi
tra-TA-yen-nee-ah rose-ah-LESS-eye

Triceratops
tri-SERR-uh-tops

Tsintaosaurus
sin-tau-SORE-us

Tyrannosaurus rex
tye-RAN-oh-SORE-us

Utahraptor
YOO-tah-RAP-tore

Velociraptor
veh-LOSS-ih-RAP-tore

Yutyrannus huali
you-tye-RAN-us hoo-all-ee

Zuul crurivastator
ZOO-ool cruh-uh-VASS-ta

Boldface indicates illustrations.

Published by National Geographic Partners, LLC. All rights reserved. Reproduction of the whole or any part of the contents without written permission from the publisher is prohibited.

Since 1888, the National Geographic Society has funded more than 12,000 research, exploration, and preservation projects around the world. The Society receives funds from National Geographic Partners, LLC, funded in part by your purchase. A portion of the proceeds from this book supports this vital work. To learn more, visit natgeo.com/info.

NATIONAL GEOGRAPHIC and Yellow Border Design are trademarks of the National Geographic Society, used under license.

For more information, visit nationalgeographic .com, call 1-877-873-6846, or write to the following address:

National Geographic Partners
1145 17th Street N.W.
Washington, DC 20036-4688 U.S.A.

Visit us online at nationalgeographic.com/books

For librarians and teachers: nationalgeographic .com/books/librarians-and-educators

More for kids from National Geographic: natgeokids.com

National Geographic Kids magazine inspires children to explore their world with fun yet educational articles on animals, science, nature, and more. Using fresh storytelling and amazing photography, *Nat Geo Kids* shows kids ages 6 to 14 the fascinating truth about the world—and why they should care. **kids.nationalgeographic.com/subscribe**

For rights or permissions inquiries, please contact National Geographic Books Subsidiary Rights: bookrights@natgeo.com

Designed by Chad Tomlinson

Trade paperback ISBN: 978-1-4263-3750-5
Reinforced library binding ISBN: 978-1-4263- 3751-2

The publisher would like to thank Julie Beer, author and researcher; Michelle Harris, author and researcher; Grace Hill, project manager; Kathryn Williams, project editor; Kathryn Robbins, art director; Hillary Leo, photo editor; Sarah J. Mock, senior photo editor; and Anne LeongSon and Gus Tello, production assistants.

Printed in Malaysia
19/IVM/1

PHOTO CREDITS

ASP = Alamy Stock Photo; GI = Getty Images; SS = Shutterstock

Cover, spine, and back cover (all), Franco Tempesta; 2, Roger Harris/Science Photo Library/GI; 4, Warpaint/SS; 6, Jon Bilous/Dreamstime; 7 (UP LE), Kovalchuk Oleksandr/SS; 7 (dino), Herschel Hoffmeyer/SS; 7 (RT), Etaphop photo/SS; 7 (LO LE), bestv/SS; 8 (UP), Artbox/SS; 8 (LO), Scisetti Alfio/SS; 9, Franco Tempesta; 10 (LE), Kirayonak Yuliya/SS; 10–11, Copyrighted by BHIGR and provided courtesy of Hammacher Schlemmer; 12, MilousSK/SS; 13 (BACK), antonpix/SS; 14 (LE), NASA Images/SS; 14 (RT), Lukassek/SS; 15, Felix Choo/ASP; 17, Franco Tempesta; 18–19, sruilk/SS; 20, yevgeniy11/SS; 21 (UP), maryartist/SS; 21 (LO), MiloVad/SS; 22, Gordon Mills/ASP; 23, Spike Malin/SWNS; 24 (I F), Christina Li/SS; 24 (RT), Corey Ford/Stocktrek Images/GI; 25, Franco Tempesta; 26, Franco Tempesta; 27 (LE), stockphoto mania/SS; 27 (tail), Warpaint/SS; 28, Catmando/SS; 29 (UP), Linda Bucklin/SS; 29 (LO), Veleknez/Dreamstime; 30, Mikkel Juul Jensen/Bonnier Publications/Science Source; 31 (UP), Maksim Ankuda/SS; 31 (LE), Saranai/SS; 32 (LE), Atalvi/Dreamstime; 32 (RT), ABC/Photofest; 33, aniko gerendi enderle/SS; 34–35, Warpaint/SS; 36, nmnac01/Adobe Stock; 37, Jim Lane/ASP; 38, iStockphoto/GI; 39, guentermanaus/SS; 40, Artens/SS; 41 (UP), iunewind/SS; 41 (LO), Michael Rosskothen/SS; 41 (court), Oleksii Sidorov/SS; 42-43, Catmando/SS; 44 (UP), Angela Coppola/Hasbro; 44 (LO LE), vi73/SS; 45 (UP), courtesy Embassy of the Netherlands; 45 (stamps), josep perianes jorba/SS; 46, UncommonGoods; 47 (LE), mjaud/SS; 47 (RT), Nerthuz/SS; 48 (LE), Catmando/SS; 48 (RT), jaroslava V/SS; 49, Javier Brosch/SS; 50 (UP LE), dive-hive/SS; 50 (UP RT), Kletr/SS; 50 (LO RT), smuay/SS; 50 (LO LE), Chatchai.wa/SS; 51 (UP), Hotshotsworldwide/Dreamstime; 51 (LO), nattaman726/SS; 52, DM7/SS; 53 (BACK), Irina Bg/SS; 53 (LO LE), Moises Fernandez Acosta/SS; 54 (UP), Linda Bucklin/SS; 54 (LO), Franco Tempesta; 55 (UP), Franco Tempesta; 55 (LO), Noiel/SS; 57, Leonello Calvetti/Stocktrek Images/GI; 58-59, Warpaintcobra/GI; 60, Herschel Hoffmeyer/SS; 61, Michael Mancuso/Times of Trenton; 62-63, Daniel Eskridge/SS; 64, Stockdreams/Dreamstime; 65, Franco Tempesta; 66 (LE), Dotted Yeti/SS; 66 (RT), Jiri Hera/SS; 67, Ksenia Bilodedenko/SS; 68, Dustin Bradford/GI; 69, photaslic/SS; 70–71 (UP), Allies Interactive/SS; 70–71 (LO), Catmando/SS; 72, Natural History Museum of Los Angeles; 73, Yoshio Tsunoda/AFLO/Newscom; 74–75, Masato Hattori; 77 (UP), Education Images/Universal Images/GI; 77 (LO), Kuttelvaserova Stuchelova/SS; 78, Masato Hattori; 79, dangdumrong/GI; 80, Paultons Park; 81, ScreenProd/Photononstop/ASP; 82, tanuha2001/SS; 83, Susan Garrett Photography; 84–85, Dariush M/SS; 86 (LE), The Royal Canadian Mint; 86 (RT), PrimoPiano/SS; 87, imageBROKER/ASP; 88, Carol Barrington/ASP; 88 (texture), Goosefrol/SS; 89 (tag), Brand X; 90–91, Catmando/SS; 91, Nerthuz/SS; 92, Sarit Wuttisan/SS; 93 (UP), Ralf Juergen Kraft/SS; 93 (LO RT), nikkytok/SS; 93 (LO LE), panbazil/SS; 94, Sweetosaur; 95 (UP), Nobumichi Tamura/Stocktrek Images/GI; 95 (LO), Ingram; 96–97, Mark Garlick/Science Photo Library/GI; 96, Mark Garlick/Science Photo Library/GI; 98, Franco Tempesta; 99 (UP LE), Roman Mirskiy, Mirskiy Art Gallery Etsy; 99 (UP RT), Lisa A/SS; 100 (LE), Aleksandar Grozdanovski/SS;

100 (RT), Esther van Hulsen; 102 (UP), Uncle Leo/SS; 102 (LO RT), jeep5d/SS; 102 (LO LE), Roman Garcia Mora/Stocktrek Images/GI; 103, Joel Sartore, National Geographic Photo Ark/National Geographic Image Collection; 104, Franco Tempesta; 105 (UP), Nobumichi Tamura/Stocktrek Images/GI; 105 (LO), MIMOgo/SS; 106–107, Tim Whitby/ASP; 107 (UP RT), Eric Isselee/SS; 108–109, Reuters/Carlo Allegri/Newscom; 110 (UP), Catmando/SS; 110 (LO), Pretty Vectors/SS; 111, Michael Rosskothen/SS; 112 (UP), Xinhua/Jin Yu/Newscom; 112 (LO), Irantzu Arbaizagoitia/SS; 113 (UP), didden/SS; 113 (LO), Malika Keehl/SS; 114 (LE), Gl0ck/SS; 114 (RT), Rubies Costume Company courtesy of Chewy; 115, vinap/SS; 116 (dino), Ton Bangkeaw/SS; 116 (RT), Tgraphic/SS; 117 (UP), Damsea/SS; 117 (LO), Michael Rosskothen/SS; 118, nexus 7/SS; 119 (LE), Franco Tempesta; 119 (RT), Winston Link/SS; 120, Mark Stevenson/Stocktrek Images/GI; 121, Stocktrek Images, Inc./ASP; 122 (LE), Franco Tempesta; 122 (RT), bildbroker.de/ASP; 124–125, Marstar/SS; 126 (LF), Rostik Solonenko/SS, 126 (RT), Jonathan Blair/GI, 127, MicroOne/SS; 128, Franco Tempesta; 129 (UP), Shujaa_777/SS; 129 (egg), Egor Rodynchenko/SS; 129 (muffs), Laborant/SS; 129 (scarf), Africa Studio/SS; 130–131, Julian Eales/ASP; 132 (LE), Ozja/SS, 132 (UP), DM7/SS; 132 (glasses), Igor Klimov/SS; 133, Eric Isselee/SS; 134, Daria Medvedeva/SS; 135 (LE), Franco Tempesta; 135 (RT), Columbia/Everett Collection, Inc.; 136, Stocktrek Images, Inc./ASP; 138 (LE), stocksolutions/SS; 138–139, Power And Syred/Science Photo Library/GI; 140 (dino), Dorling Kindersley; 140 (BACK), lilalove/SS; 141 (UP), moomsabuy/SS; 142-143, Peter Phipp/Travelshots/ASP; 144, courtesy of Mark Verge a.k.a. Jungle Jack; 145 (UP), Franco Tempesta; 145 (court), Es sarawuth/SS; 145 (LO), KittyVector/ShutterPoint Photography; 146, Sudowoodo/SS; 147 (LO), James Kuether; 148 (UP), Ritu Manoj Jethani/SS; 148 (LO), Anita Ponne/SS; 149, Ben Stevens/i-Images/ZUMA Wire/Newscom; 150 (LE), Stocktrek Images, Inc./ASP; 150 (RT), Linda Bucklin/SS; 151, DM7/SS; 152, Olga Popova/SS; 153 (UP), Photodisc; 153 (LO), abrakadabra/SS; 154 (UP LE), Stocktrek Images, Inc./ASP; 154 (RT), Universal Images Group North America LLC/ASP; 155, courtesy of Tovolo; 156, Elenarts/SS; 157, Catmando/SS; 158, Franco Tempesta; 159, Aksana/SS; 160, Mick Cluley of Shpangle Jewellery; 161, Victor Habbick/SS; 162, Ian Dagnall/ASP; 163, chemonk/SS; 164, Selenka/Dreamstime; 165, Anan Kaewkhammul/SS; 166, Franco Tempesta; 167 (LE), world of vector/SS; 167 (RT), Franco Tempesta; 168 (LE), NG Images/ASP; 168 (RT), Cheung Chungtat; 169, Tronin Andrei/SS; 170, Landry's Inc.; 171 (UP), neftali/SS; 171 (LO), Butterfly Hunter/SS; 172–173, Herschel Hoffmeyer/SS; 174, Emily Jaschke; 176, Robert Clark/National Geographic Image Collection; 177 (UP), SmileKorn/SS; 177 (LO), Daniel Eskridge/SS; 178 (LE), Franco Tempesta; 178 (RT), SofiaV/SS; 179 (UP), Stocktrek Images/Science Source; 179 (LO), SIRIOH Co., LTD/ASP; 180 (UP), JHVEPhoto/SS; 180 (LO), Jarva Jar/SS; 181 (RT), Alhovik/SS; 182 (LE), Red Confidential/SS; 182 (RT), Anna Hoychuk/SS; 183, Victor Virgile/Gamma-Rapho/GI; 184, DM7/SS; 186, MicroOne/SS; 187 (UP), Jonathan Harbourne/ASP; 187 (LO), Dudarev Mikhail/SS; 188, Corey Ford/GI; 189, Scott Beseler; 190, Leandro Henrich/ASP; 191 (UP), Royal Saskatchewan Museum (RSM/R.C. McKellar); 191 (LO), Tom McHugh/Science Source; 192–193, Eugen Thome/Dreamstime; 194, Foxyliam/SS; 195, pencil artist/SS; 196–197, wwing/GI

BLAST FROM THE PAST!

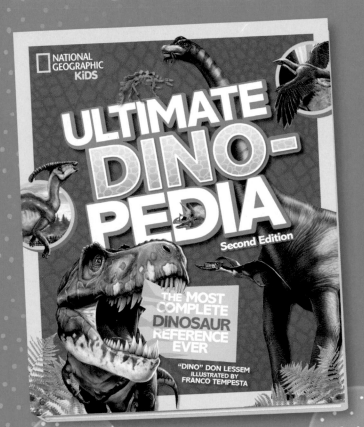

WANT MORE COOL INFO ABOUT THESE INCREDIBLE CREATURES?

Get the most amazing dinosaur reference book, chock-full of fascinating profiles, colorful illustrations, fun facts, and more.